AMERICAN VOYAGE

AMERICAN VOYAGE

Photographs By Mario Carnicelli

REEL ART PRESS

DAVID HILL GALLERY

For Nicla and Chiara

If Mario Carnicelli hadn't closed his photography store in 2010 and asked me to have a look at his old negatives I would never have known, like many of us, that he was a photographer. In his cellar lay a hidden treasure, a foreign and fascinating world in black and white but also in exquisite colour, hundreds of stories and microstories of the sixties and seventies mostly set in Italy, but also in America.

Once we started curating and scanning the archive of carelessly stored medium format and 35mm negatives, the nostalgic vintage flavour made way for the discovery of an astonishingly modern attitude, beauty without rhetoric, ordinary gestures that become iconic, centered on his interest in exploring the human condition of individuals in different societies. His archive comprises a cohesive body of documentary work of thousands of images, that after fifty years finally gets the attention it deserves.

BÄRBEL REINHARD

Bärbel Reinhard called me to consult and help her plan ways of showcasing the newly rediscovered work of Mario Carnicelli. When I first saw his photographs, especially the contacts of his American Voyage, I was completely surprised by how modern his images were, especially in colour, and with an almost un-Italian gaze. They did not compare to any other work done in the same period in Italy.

A peculiar characteristic of Carnicelli's modernity lies in what he defines as an approach of normality versus his subjects, registering what he finds in front of his camera, without intervening. An atypical attitude for a kind of photography that at the time was still looking for artistic authoritativeness in the decisive moment and in composition. Mario Carnicelli comes to attention not only in the history of Italian photography but also internationally, precisely for the modality and the era in which he worked.

MARCO SIGNORINI

Photography is my way of writing, my language. My main subject is always the person, the humanity. Man is never alone, he is the crowd and the crowd becomes man. People narrate their selves through their gaze, their clothes, their way of moving. You understand immediately where they come from and where they are going. Images come to me as if they were looking for me, they don't need footnotes, just references: place and date. It's in this precise moment that an image becomes a photograph.

MARIO CARNICELLI

In 1966, Mario Carnicelli—at the time a young documentary photographer from Tuscany—won first place in a national Italian photography competition sponsored by *Popular Photography* magazine, Ferrania Film, Mamiya and Pentax. On submitting an image of a demonstration in his hometown of Pistoia, Tuscany, Carnicelli won a scholarship to photograph America. He left Europe for the first time and embarked on a one month trip to the States, his American Voyage. This was followed by more trips over the next few years, and time spent in cities including Detroit, Washington, D.C., San Francisco, Buffalo, New York and Chicago.

Carnicelli was attracted by the carefree liberty, the happy-go-lucky spirit of American society and was overwhelmed by its diversity, mix of cultures, traditions, ways of life, and by the extroverted fashion and individualism. Seen through the prism of his own Italian heritage—a homogenous national identity tied to an idea of collective membership and strong familial bonds—he perceived the complexity of the melting pot of American society with an alert and acute gaze. America was more than another continent, another part of the world; America was a state of mind, a passion, a restless fever. Everything was possible and everything could change from one moment to the next.

The photographs that Carnicelli brought back from his first trip were showcased in an exhibition at the Pirelli Tower in Milan under the rather curious title, *I'm sorry, America!* Carnicelli was apologizing for the lens of an outsider, presenting everyday life in America from an inquisitive and very personal point of view. He felt almost like an intruder in a society completely new to him. With no preconceptions of the American Dream, his work also revealed its contradictions, loneliness and its insurmountable class and social divisions. This deep and fundamental fascination brought him back to the States over the next few years, always with an anthropological focus, interested in ordinary people, in everyday life.

In Carnicelli's work as a freelance photojournalist he also travelled to other countries, working on both commissions and personal projects. In the early 1970s, however, he renounced this career to follow in the footsteps of the family business as a dealer of photographic equipment, opening a renowned developing and printing service in Florence.

The regret of having abandoned his vocation was always with Carnicelli. He was again *sorry, America!*, this time for giving up on his photographic vision, his lost dream; for having forgotten thousands of negatives in a box in the cellar for over fifty years.

AMERICAN VOYAGE

Telephone booths, O'Hare International Airport, Chicago, 1966

Check-in counter, O'Hare International Airport, Chicago, 1966

Passengers, O'Hare International Airport, Chicago, 1966

Cafeteria counter, O'Hare International Airport, Chicago, 1966

Job centre, Chicago, 1966

Yellow cab, Chicago, 1966

Barber College, Chicago, 1966

Job centre line, Chicago, 1966

Factories, Chicago, 1966

Salem cigarettes billboard, Chicago, 1966

Win A '67 Car!, Chicago, 1966

Model at hairdresser convention, Chicago, 1966

Hairdresser convention, Chicago, 1966

Wig stand, Chicago, 1966

Green 1955 Ford, Chicago, 1966

No Parking, Chicago, 1966

Bus to Indiana, Chicago, 1966

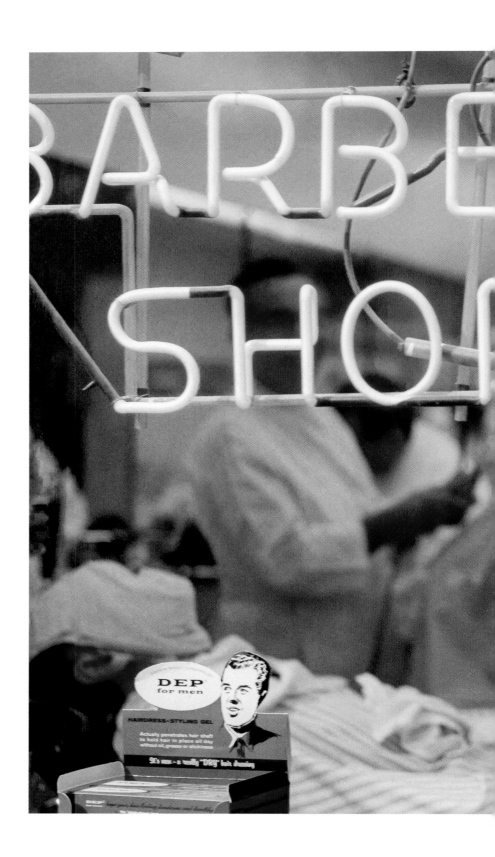

Barber shop neon, Chicago, 1966

Red lights, Chicago, 1966

After work, Chicago, 1966

South Pacific restaurant, Chicago, 1966

Club 606, Chicago, 1966

Vote, Detroit, 1966

Ford Car Expo, Detroit, 1966

Retired trade union worker, Detroit, 1966

Police, Detroit, 1966

Retired trade union workers, Detroit, 1966

Photographer's studio, Boston, 1966

Football players, Boston, 1966

Marines, Boston, 1966

Jewellery store, Dallas, 1967

Police car, Dallas, 1967

Anti-war demonstration, Dallas, 1967

Anti-war demonstration, Dallas, 1967

Neo-Nazi demonstrator, Dallas, 1967

Neo-Nazi speaker, Dallas, 1967

$1 photo, Dallas, 1967

Neiman Marcus, Dallas, 1967

Lazy hour, El-Paso, 1967

Newspaper seller, El-Paso, 1967

After work stroll, Washington D.C., 1966

Two girls in a car, Washington D.C., 1966

Bus stop, Washington D.C., 1966

Bus station, Washington D.C., 1966

Evening Star seller, Washington D.C., 1966

Lincoln Memorial, Washington D.C., 1967

Lincoln Memorial, Washington D.C., 1967

President Kennedy Gravesite, Washington D.C., 1966

Tourists at the Eternal Flame, Washington D.C., 1966

Well-dressed lady, San Francisco, 1967

Couple, San Francisco, 1967

Hippie, San Francisco, 1967

Painter, San Francisco, 1967

NAACP, Los Angeles, 1967

Parking lot, Los Angeles, 1967

After school, Buffalo, 1966

Red door, Stanford, 1966

Immigrants, Buffalo, 1966

Kids, Buffalo, 1966

Auto shop, Buffalo, 1966

Bus stop, Buffalo, 1966

Schoolboy, New York, 1966

Primary school, New York, 1966

Fashion students, New York, 1966

Wig store, New York, 1966

Nurses outfitters, New York, 1966

Newsstand, New York, 1966

Museum of Modern Art, New York, 1967

Cartier, New York, 1967

Traffic lights 1, New York, 1967

Traffic lights 2, New York, 1967

Beggar, New York, 1966

Entrepreneurs, New York, 1966

A kiss in the park, New York, 1966

Motorbike rider, New York, 1966

Bus riders, New York, 1967

Telephone booths, New York, 1966

Subway, New York, 1967

Subway entrance, New York, 1966

Ladies at movie premiere, Broadway, New York, 1966

Movie premiere, Broadway, New York, 1966

Blind date, New York, 1966

Village Varieties, New York, 1966

42nd Street at night, New York, 1966

Black '67 Plymouth Belvedere, Brooklyn, New York, 1967

Grocery store, Brooklyn, New York, 1966

Grocery shopping, Harlem, New York, 1966

Nation of Islam bookstore, Harlem, New York, 1966

Lady in fur leaving pizzeria, New York, 1969

Hair stylists, New York, 1969

Man in a car window, New York, 1969

People are the ultimate spectacle, New York, 1969

Street at night, Washington D.C., 1969

Aunt Edonide, Stanford, 1969

Hat seller, New York, 1969

I would first of all like to thank Tony Nourmand of Reel Art Press and David Hill of David Hill Gallery for making *American Voyage* possible.

Special thanks to the curator of my archive and my work Bärbel Reinhard and Marco Signorini for their help.

I also want to thank Luigina Murgia, Danilo Montanari, Samuele Bertinelli, Elena Testaferrata, Mariano Cipollini, Massimo Pantano, and Francesco Carnicelli.

in memory of Vincenzo and my parents.

David Hill Gallery would like to thank Alex Schneideman at Flow Photographic for his skillful work in bringing these wonderful images to life.

Captions for Opening Pages: p.2 Mario Carnicelli with construction workers, New York, 1966; p.5 Crowd watching television in shop window, New York, 1967; p.6 Airport barbershop, Chicago, 1966; p.9 Mario Carnicelli with Mamiya Universal 6x9 camera, New York, 1966; p.10 View from hotel window, Chicago, 1966; p.12 Mario Carnicelli with Hasselblad 500C camera, Dallas, 1967; p.14-15 Bus stop, Buffalo, 1966; p.16 double exposure, New York, 1966

Editors: Tony Nourmand and David Hill

Curator of the Mario Carnicelli Archive: Bärbel Reinhard

Consultant: Marco Signorini

Art Direction and Design: Joakim Olsson

Text Editor: Alison Elangasinghe

Editorial Assistant: Rory Bruton

First published 2018 by Reel Art Press/David Hill Gallery

Reel Art Press is an imprint of Rare Art Press Ltd., London, UK

www.reelartpress.com

First Edition

10 9 8 7 6 5 4 3 2 1

ISBN: 978-1-909526-57-0

Printed by Graphius, Gent